The Universal Vacuum Cleaner

OXFORD
UNIVERSITY PRESS

Great Clarendon Street, Oxford OX2 6DP

Oxford University Press is a department of the University of Oxford.
It furthers the University's objective of excellence in research, scholarship,
and education by publishing worldwide in

Oxford   New York

Auckland   Cape Town   Dar es Salaam   Hong Kong   Karachi
Kuala Lumpur   Madrid   Melbourne   Mexico City   Nairobi
New Delhi   Shanghai   Taipei   Toronto

With offices in

Argentina   Austria   Brazil   Chile   Czech Republic   France   Greece
Guatemala   Hungary   Italy   Japan   Poland   Portugal   Singapore
South Korea   Switzerland   Thailand   Turkey   Ukraine   Vietnam

Oxford is a registered trade mark of Oxford University Press
in the UK and in certain other countries

British Library Cataloguing in Publication Data

Data available

ISBN-13: 978-0-19-276313-6
ISBN-10: 0-19-276313-X

3 5 7 9 10 8 6 4 2

Typeset by Mary Tudge (Typesetting Services)

Printed in Great Britain by
Cox & Wyman Ltd, Reading, Berkshire

The Universal Vacuum Cleaner

and other riddle poems

Compiled by John Foster

Illustrated by Tony Ross

OXFORD

UNIVERSITY PRESS

Contents

Hey Diddle Riddle

John Foster

Hey diddle riddle
My first is in first,
But isn't in fiddle.
My second is in kitten,
But not found in cat.
And my third and my fourth
Aren't in this or in that!
But they are in the middle
Of middle and muddle
And my fifth and my sixth
Both end little and puddle.

If you're still in a puzzle
To know how I look
You'll find me as you turn
Each page of this book.

I Leap and Dance

Cynthia Rider

I leap and dance,
I flicker and prance,
I am buried deep in the earth.
I lie hidden in trees
I am fanned by the breeze,
Flint and stone can give me birth.
I give comfort and cheer
When used with care,
But when out of control I bring danger—beware!

A Slippery Customer

Kate Williams

It has no shape, yet it shapes the land.
It has no size, yet it fits anything.
It has no legs, yet it runs everywhere.
It has no voice, yet it murmurs and hums.
It has no colour, yet it seems to have them all.
It has no muscles, yet it can hold up ships.
It has no flavour, yet we drink it every day.
It has no mind, yet it likes to have its way,
and however you get rid of it,
it's sure to still be there, somewhere,
so beware . . .

2

What's There?

Gina Douthwaite

Raging crazily round the roof
as though in torture from a tooth
this uninvited guest gyrates,
cracks creaking beams, whips under slates,
prises open trapdoor jaws,
pads across cold bedroom floors,
rattles handles,
battles
with doors,

hides in curtains, whines and *s-i-g-h-s*,
scrapes at skin with tongues of ice,
SCREAMS down chimneys *startling* flames.
Hear restless voices wailing names?
Hoaxing, coaxing from the stair,
calling cats that bristle hair,
cower and yowl
at what? . . .

What's there
    raging crazily round the roof?
They say they know
    —but where's the proof?

What's the Game?

Eric Finney

Long walks in this game:
No hurry, just a stroll.
Shoot a white ball
Down a small hole.

Short walks in this game.
Here are the clues:
Cushions, pockets,
Breaks, and cues.

Use a piece of wood
To defend three sticks,
You might score four—
Or even six.

Love's nothing in this game.
Take careful aim,
Toss the ball up and whack it
Over the net with a racket.

Two games:
One with thirty players,
The other with four less.
All players often end up
A mighty muddy mess.

Riddleferee

Daphne Kitching

I whistle while I work,
While I work I play cards,
My red means go not stop,
I receive no payment for the kicks I give,
People like them and want more,
My helpers run on lines and are trained,
I take part in games
But never win, never lose,
I start and finish,
Time is in my hands.

IT('s a) Riddle

Daphne Kitching

Log on with no danger of burning,
My mouse eats no cheese,
My web has no spiders
My net catches no fish,
Surf without sea
If you recognize me.

What in the World?

Ian Bland

I'm a world-exploring bunch of words
Just looking for a home,

I'm a message-giving lightning bolt
Of electric information,

I'm a computer-dwelling missive
Clogging up your files and folders,

I'm a telephone-transmitting mass
Of ideas, jokes, and pictures,

World-exploring
Message-giving
Computer-dwelling
Telephone-transmitting,

What in the world am I?

Seaside

Andrew Detheridge

gout hips oriz
n a s o h o
looki tthe nthe nalways

makesmewant t o f l y a w a y

like the gulls h o e i g v r e d
v r n o e h a

I love to c a t c crabs ⚡ with my net

in the s l i m y and s i p r rock pools
l p e y

then until it's o v e r f l o w i n g

crabs and seaweed
lots of shells and
with lots and
my bucket
fill

and my mum **screams** really loudly
when I put some seaweed on her belly!

Riddles of the Seashore

Catherine Benson

Tossed into tangles by waves
it drizzles salt-sparkle onto sand.

?

Soft under seaweed the toe-nipper
waits for new armour.

?

Pentagram on the beach,
fish with a sky-name.

?

Not for collecting or poking,
leave this jellymould body for the tide.

?

In a bowl of barnacled rock a tiny sea
covers sea-flowers, shrimps, and a crab.

?

Written in the sand, a seagull's poem
is rubbed out by waves.

?

As far as the eye can see, scallops
of white embroidery on grey-blue and blue-green.

?

Holding secret sea-songs and carried home,
it spills music into my ear.

?

Silk and Satin

Barbara Moore

The silk and satin of my sheen
Would make a present for a queen;
But who could guess my lowly start?
A piece of grit lies at my heart.

Pale Satellite

Marian Swinger

Pale satellite, silvering
the clouds that she rides,
her finery borrowed,
the mistress of tides.

Riddle of the Fairground

Moira Andrew

I stand as tall as a mountain.
    Only the brave climb
        my straight steep path,
      to join the river of screaming children,
    to look down on parents,
crawling like insects, far below.
    I push children off my clifftop
        to fall swirling, whirling,
           head-first, feet-first, gushing,
        rushing round my rocky sides
    in a torrent of excitement
till they land gasping at my feet.

What am I?

Chin-sticker, Lip-gripper

Judith Nicholls

I am light as a breeze,
a puff of pink smoke;
a chin-sticker, lip-gripper,
fluffy pink joke!

I cling to your fingers,
I curl round your thumb;
then like a small duvet
I wrap round your tongue.

Christmas Riddles

John Cotton

(1)
My slender figure charms,
Dressed in white or bright colours.
The frills of my dress grow and gather
As I grow smaller,
Lighting your celebratory tree.
A comfort in the darkness,
A small welcoming warmth.

(2)
A steaming richness,
A fruity companion,
A cannon ball not for firing
Though I sometimes flame.
I complete your feast
With my green buttonhole
And yellow waistcoat.

(3)
Watery bones,
Transparent pencils,
Cold fingers pointing out from the eaves,
A fringe of lances.

(4)
Brightly dressed mysteries,
Joyous surprises and exciters of hopes,
Tokens of love,
Affection's messengers,
Containing annual delights.

(5)
Sent from the corners of the round world,
A blue uniformed messenger delivers them.
Small pictures of friendship,
Making a mantelshelf gallery of goodwill.

(6)
I am busy when you are abed.
I feel strange in my disguise,
Like an oversize robin
That has been out in the snow.
I creep stealthily to avoid detection
Although I know I am welcome.

(7)
Rain polishes
My round-the-year gloss,
Honing my row of sharp spears.
In winter I come into my own
Bearing the crown
And gifts
Of bright beads of blood.

Santa's Mystery Letters

Clare Bevan

Which animals wrote these letters—and forgot to sign them?

1. Santa—please send me
   Some brand new PJs.
   I'm sick of my stripes
   And their black-and-white
   ways.
   I'm keen to be spotted,
   So let's start a craze
   For dazzling patterns
   To brighten my days.

2. Dear Father Christmas,
   I'm not one to grumble
   But I WISH that my voice
   Sounded less like a rumble
   And more like a flute,
   Or a sweet, trilling song
   To ring through the woods
   As I trundle along.
   (P.S. Maybe also
   A cool, summer coat
   With a little less fur
   Round my paws and my
   throat?)

3. Dear Santa, I'm hoping
   For face cream (the best)
   To rub in my wrinkles,
   To smooth on my chest,
   To tighten the skin
   Round my neck and my
   knees,
   And to soften my spike . . .
   So bring TONS of it please.

4. Dear Santa, I'm writing
   To ask for new teeth
   That aren't quite so pointy
   And sharp underneath,
   But cuter and shinier,
   Not so alarming,
   So I'm less like Count
   Dracula—
   More like Prince Charming.

16

Win
ter
Rid
dle

Matt Black

Soft
  as
  feathers,

cool as
  drops
  of milk,

in flurries
  fluttering
  like

  dancing
circles of
  silk,

  like drifting
confetti of
  white   lace,

I'm a soft
  veil of
  winter—

floating
  over
your
  face

Two Cinquain Riddles

Great Cat

Marian Swinger

Great cat,
muscles rippling
beneath smooth golden fur,
striped terror, will you, too, join the
dodo?

Ship of the Desert

Marian Swinger

It spits,
a splay footed,
hump-backed beast of burden.
We greet the ship of the desert.
Salaam.

A Cross Stick in Disguise

Damian Harvey

Crawling hunter by the water's edge with
Reptilian eyes, keen and sharp,
Observing all that moves.
Camouflaged perfectly, blending in, this
Oppressor of the river,
Disguised as a log, drifts on by. Completely
Invisible to the casual eye, it
Lurks in the shallows with its
Evil piano-like grin, sharp and white, ready to strike.

Upside Down

Jane Clarke

I live in trees
And hang around,
My feet are rarely
On the ground.

My hair is long
And I'm so slow,
Mould covers me
From head to toe.

My earth is blue,
My sky is brown.
I see the world
From upside down.

Scuttle-bug

Judith Nicholls

Scuttle-bug,
shadow-foot,
bringer of night;
sky without stars,
obsidian-light;
shiny as coal,
new-mined and still bright;
smooth as new carbon,
dark and untyped.

20

What Is He?

Liz Brownlee

His back is humpy,
he can be freckled or stripy and speckled,
his face is grumpy,
he can be blotted or patchy and dotted,
but he cannot be spotted.
his toes are curled,
his tail is furled,

Without Wings

Tim Pointon

Flying
high without a
single wing, like a bird
but I never sing. Floating over
towns, trains and trees, fields,
farms and factories, while below
toy figures point and stare
as I drift through clouds
which announce me
with a silent
fanfare.

Under me sits
a fire in a casket

and, even lower,
little people in
a little basket.

The Clue's Up There!

Tim Pointon

You won't
find a spoon lying in me
and, what's more, there is no cup
to see. I'm not made of fine bone china, nor do I grace the table
of the greatest ocean liner. Finally, if inside me you peered, you might
think my passengers looked rather weird!

All Year Round

Fred Sedgwick

All year round
it is a rooted column,
a climbing frame.

In spring
it is a tower block for nests
wearing a huge green dress.

Summer comes. It hides
sky and almost everything

and in autumn
it drops gold on my path.

Winter.
It is a black bony creature
sometimes wearing
white underwear.

All year round
it is a rooted column,
a climbing frame.

Spring Flower Riddle

David Whitehead

Our golden trumpets shout loud and strong—
 Winter's gone! Spring won't be long!

On grassy banks our prim, creamy flowers
 Bring a burst of colour after April's showers.

As our simple wintry name implies—
 A fall of crystal whiteness from the skies.

Tiny goblets of yellow, mauve, and blue—
 These little cups collect the morning dew.

Million upon million tiny fairy bells
 Make a bright blue carpet in the woodland dells.

We grow by the roadside, sun-yellow flowers.
 When our petals are gone we blow away the hours.

Tiny white stars chain-stitched across the lawn.
 Called the day's eye; wide-eyed from early dawn.

Hiding in the woodland, shy and tiny by the hedge.
 Sweet-scented—I'm a colour at the rainbow's edge.

Put all together we make a spring bouquet—

But—where we live is where we love to stay.

Ready for Sun Fun

Tim Pointon

My ambition is to
see the sun, bask on the beach, and have
some fun. But I only come out when the sky is a patchwork of
greys and my owner miserably grumbles, 'Oh no! Not another one of

t
h
o
s
e
d
a
y
s.'

What Am I?

Brenda Williams

I'm a reflection
In the spray,
I am a bridge
That will not stay.
I can cross rivers,
mountains, sea.
No one ever
touches me.
I can be weak
Or I can be bold.
Follow my path
To a pot of gold.

A Cool Guy

Angela Topping

I hum in the summer kitchen,
a white box of winter. I make
ice while the sun shines. My
light flicks on and off at your
whim. In me you hide fruit of
summer, safe from the brown
menace of heat which thieves
its bloom. Water in me is like
the water from mountain pools
cooled in my frosty embrace.
I bring relief from the midday
blistering sun when you clink
my gift of ice cubes in squash.
Cool   chill.

Haiku Riddle

Celia Warren

Under the pillow
part of a six-year-old smile
left for the fairies

Two Tanka Riddles

Marian Swinger

Innumerable,
they twinkle in the sunshine
golden-white, packed tight.
Gently, as through an hourglass,
they trickle through your fingers.

What are you? A breath,
a whisper, a sweet, soft, sigh?
Trees murmur, grass sways,
you kiss my cheek, stir my hair
as you pass, gentle zephyr.

Seven Anagriddles

Eric Finney

*The answer to each riddle is also an anagram of the word or words in **bold**. In each case the answer is a single word.*

Entertainment at home—
(For which kids are gluttons!)
The **novelties** I view—
Just press the buttons!

You may think their life is ace
But kids, kids, kids are **the cares** they face.

Towards this the teacher
Slowly proceeded,
Wondering, 'Will it be **calm**—
Or SOS needed?'

The plane is a jumbo—
And this is too.
But not at the airport,
Perhaps at the zoo.

Even a **cart-horse** might think it bliss
To listen to music played by this!

I'm keen on **handouts**—are there any?
Yes, quite a lot. This tells how many.

Shout, **then scream**
For your favourite team—
Get thoroughly excited.
But which one here
Will you support:
City or United?

What Is the Cat's Name?

Colin Macfarlane

(1)
He likes to stay up half the night
and sleep for half the day;
ready for a noisy fight
or even just to play . . .
look closely at this riddle,
did I give his name away?

(2)
This kitty-cat's name is easily found,
so listen carefully . . . swap around!
It isn't the least like Simon or Jenny
and, just as a footnote, you haven't got any!

Crumbs

Roger Stevens

My first is in baker and also in bread
My second's in miller and also in bread
My third is in cake and also in bread
My fourth is in wrapper and also in bread
My last is in doughnut and also in bread.

My whole thing is found
Near the mouth, more or less,
And you often find crumbs there.
What am I? Can you guess?

Make a Quick Guess

Coral Rumble

My first is in swim but not in beneath,
My second's in hungry and also in teeth.
My third's in attack but isn't in blood,
My fourth's in rip but not in thud.
My fifth is in killer but isn't in cruel—
I can see you right now and I'm starting to drool.

Word Works

Mary Green

Find the letter for each verse and make the word.

I am in speak but not in tell,
I am in whisper but not in yell,
I am in peel but not in bell,
And you'll find me in spin as well as spell.

I am in loyal but not in true,
I am in gold but not in blue,
I am in hold but not in glue,
I am in know but not in knew.

I am in grave but not in tomb,
I am in space but not in room,
I am in flower but not in bloom,
I am in death but not in doom.

My last is in mighty and yet not great,
You'll find me in Molly but not in Kate,
I'm never in yak and never in you,
But always in rhyme and poem too!

The Poem and the Poet

Rachel Rooney

The chicken comes before the egg
A frog before its spawn
The plant must come before the seed
And deers before their fawn
But mums come after boys and girls
As if you didn't know it!
So can you tell me which comes first
The poem or the poet?

My Word

Trevor Parsons

Starts with a letter in fourth but not author,
its second you'll find in fifth but not froth,
its third is in third but is not there in thinned,
the fourth is in second but never in conned,
the fifth is in sixth but not in six hundred.
The whole wins the race, is what comes before all.

A Fortunate Word

John Foster

The first of you comes last of all
And the last of all is first.
The last of you is second too
And the third of second is third.
The first of key is second to last
And so is the last of unlock.

Solve this puzzle and you'll see
How fortunate a word can be.

Who's Who in School?

Melissa Lawrence

Spud basher
Mince hasher
Soup pourer
Apple corer
Pudding mixer
Menu fixer
Who am I?

Dirt sweeper
Key keeper
Locker mender
Boiler tender
Sick remover
Corridor hooverer
Who am I?

Whistle blower
Tantrum thrower
Kit inspector
Excuse detector
Football pumper
Hurdle jumper
Who am I?

Headmaster minder
Stationery finder
Parent ringer
Tea bringer
Visitor walker
Telephone talker
Who am I?

A Riddle for the Teacher

Granville Lawson

I'm sure you'll like this funny riddle
It ends at the start
And begins in *the* middle
It's not the best, it's not the *worst*
Your *teacher* ought to read it first.
In front of *the* class now loud and clear
Speak up so all the *school* can hear.
A teacher should be well equipped
To say the words in slanted script
So back to the start you're all referred
Then shout out each italic word!

Sounds of Silence?

Judith Nicholls

My words fill your head
like a chattering tongue,
though I'm mute as a marble,
silent as stone.

I cheer you or sadden,
puzzle or preach;
entertain you, persuade you,
amuse you or teach.

Paperweight, motionless,
soundless as bone . . .
yet though speechless,
not spineless: I carry
a weight of my own.

Choose me now, use me,
then set me down:
never fear, I'll be there

when you are long gone!

What Book Am I?

Debjani Chatterjee

Turn my pages, reader.
I am no ordinary book,
I am not a storyteller,
yet worth your long hard look.

An armchair traveller
can climb my mountains, swim my seas,
marvel at the range I cover,
visit many countries.

I am well-named after
a giant who shouldered the Earth.
Geography holds no terror;
In me it takes its birth.

Do You Know My Dreaded Name?

Debjani Chatterjee

I'm a huge man-eating giant,
the god Poseidon's favoured son,
no less famous than that trickster-
hero who called himself 'No one'.

Mine are a simple island folk.
We do not till, we do not reap.
We do not trade, nor build our homes,
but dwell in caves and tend our sheep.

So do you know my dreaded name?
I drink goats' milk and fine Greek wines.
I'm no teacher and have no school,
but I have one pupil who shines.

'No one' blinded me as I slept.
My roars made all my brothers run.
'Who attacks you?' they asked of me,
and I replied: 'It was No one.'

Creature of Fable

Marian Swinger

Creature of fable,
phantom of dreams,
wanderer of forests
and crystal clear streams;
a maiden may halter you,
no other can tame you.
On your brow grows the wonder
by which people name you.

The Riddle of the Sphinx

Clare Bevan

The Sphinx sprawled in the sunset
Beneath a blood-red sky,
The desert seemed to shudder
As a rider cantered by.

The Sphinx sprang like a nightmare
To bar the stranger's way,
It shook its mane of darkness,
It snarled above its prey.

'Invaders of my kingdom
Must swiftly answer me—
What creature walks on four legs,
On two legs, then on three?'

The path was white with rib bones,
The dunes were striped with death,
The Sphinx licked ragged talons
And yawned with tainted breath.

The traveller dismounted,
He soothed his trembling horse,
He crossed the sandy graveyard,
He cried, 'It's Man, of course.

At first he creeps on four legs,
In time he strides on two,
At last a stick supports him—
And yet he masters you!'

The Sphinx wailed like a kitten,
It crouched as still as stone.
The prince rode on unfettered
To face his fate alone.

Peasants, Beware!

Marian Swinger

It walks the dark woods,
Terror, its name,
its nature split two ways,
a wild and a tame.
Living in legend,
or in a bad dream,
its life spent in torment,
it's not what it seems.
Ruled by that power
which governs the tides,
it struggles against it,
cringes and hides.
It writhes and it twists,
but its cells rearrange.
Defeated once more,
it submits to the Change
and two legs are four legs,
smooth skin sprouts fur,
nose becomes muzzle,
features are blurred
and then the red slaughter,
the slash and the tear
as it rages through dark woods.
Peasants, beware!

Trick or Treat Riddle

Mike Johnson

My first letter's in werewolves—
hear their fearsome call?
My second letter is in treat,
but in trick not at all.
My third is found in monster
and it's in Martian, too;
my fourth occurs in pumpkin
(not once—there are two).
My fifth's always in witches,
but never found in warlock,
my sixth letter's in Martian
and in monster, too.
    Knock, knock.
My last letter is located
twice in Hallowe'en.

Trick or treat my riddle,
your *neck* knows, when I've been!

Who Am I?

Nick Toczek

I've always been extremely thin
Yet I contain the room I'm in
Though it's untouched by hand or din.

And I have got the smoothest skin.
It's shiny, like a fish's fin.
To look at, I could be your twin.

To find the word that's me just spin
Six letters, but you must begin
By making sure I've three Rs in.

Whatever Can It Be?

Gina Douthwaite

Follows
down the footpath,
copies every stride,
creeps around the corner
when I try to hide.
Bends along the fences,
overtakes on walls—
taller, thinner,
faster,
fatter,
slower,
small.
Underneath the lamp-post
fades
as
though
it's
shy.
L-o-n-g-s
to snuggle
into bed
when the
moon is
high. Reaches
out to touch me.
What- ever
can it be?
This thing
that's like
a twin, this
shape that
sticks with me?

The Conqueror

Marian Swinger

It can go very slowly,
but sometimes too fast.
It can make you be first
as well as be last.
We have lots or too little,
and we won't see it end.
It can destroy
but it also can mend.
It can make mountains crumble
and great cities fall
and in the end,
it conquers us all.

Universal Vacuum Cleaner

Jane Clarke

What's the matter?

A star is dying

releasing forces

terrifying.

Old red giant

huge and shiny

Collapses.

Now he's dense and tiny

Gravity

becoming meaner.

Universal

vacuum cleaner!

Index of Titles and First Lines

(First lines are in italic)

Answers to Riddles

Acknowledgements

Every effort has been made to trace and contact copyright holders before publication and we are grateful to all those who have granted us permission. We apologize for any inadvertent errors and will be pleased to rectify these at the earliest opportunity.

Moira Andrew: 'Riddle of the Fairground', copyright © Moira Andrew 2005. **Catherine Benson:** 'Riddles of the Seashore', copyright © Catherine Benson 2005. **Clare Bevan:** 'Santa's Mystery Letters' and 'The Riddle of the Sphinx', copyright © Clare Bevan 2005. **Matt Black:** 'Winter Riddle', copyright © Matt Black 2005. **Ian Bland:** 'What in the World?', copyright © Ian Bland 2005. **Liz Brownlee:** 'What Is He?', copyright © Liz Brownlee 2005. **Debjani Chatterjee:** 'What Book Am I?' and 'Do You Know My Dreaded Name?', copyright © Debjani Chatterjee 2005. **Jane Clarke:** 'Upside Down' and 'Universal Vacuum Cleaner', copyright © Jane Clarke 2005. **John Cotton:** 'Christmas Riddles', copyright © the Estate of John Cotton. **Andrew Detheridge:** 'Seaside', copyright © Andrew Detheridge 2005. **Gina Douthwaite:** 'What's There?', copyright © Gina Douthwaite 1990, first published in *Creepy Poems*, published by Usborne Publishing Ltd, used by permission of the author. 'Whatever Can It Be?' first published as 'Shadow' from *Picture a Poem*, by Gina Douthwaite, published by Hutchinson. Reprinted by permission of The Random House Group Ltd. **Eric Finney:** 'What's the Game?' and 'Seven Anagriddles', copyright © Eric Finney 2005. **John Foster:** 'Hey Diddle Riddle' and 'A Fortunate Word', copyright © John Foster 2005. **Mary Green:** 'Word Works', copyright © Mary Green 2005. **Damian Harvey:** 'A Cross Stick in Disguise', copyright © Damian Harvey 2005. **Mike Johnson:** 'Trick or Treat Riddle', copyright © Mike Johnson 2005. **Daphne Kitching:** 'Riddleferee' and 'IT('s) a Riddle', copyright © Daphne Kitching 2005. **Melissa Lawrence:** 'Who's Who in School?', copyright © Melissa Lawrence 2005. **Granville Lawson:**